THE QUEEN'S CORONATION

THE INSIDE STORY

James Wilkinson

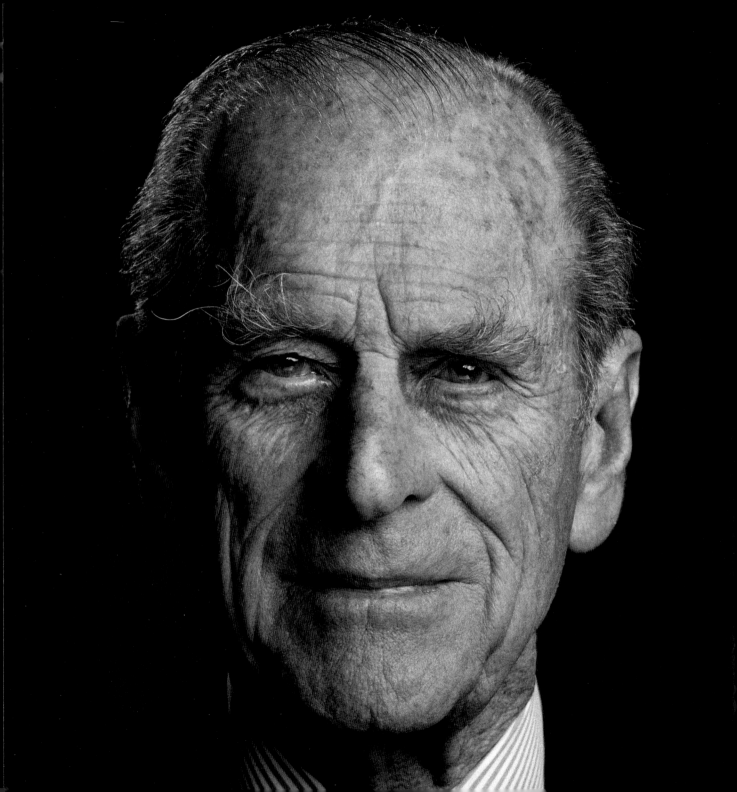

THE QUEEN'S CORONATION

THE INSIDE STORY

The Queen succeeded her father in 1952, but it is easy to forget that her Coronation only took place nearly eighteen months later. This is the story of what happened during those hectic eighteen months. Most of the people who masterminded the elaborate ceremony are no longer with us, but there are many people who took part in the events, or witnessed the ceremony in the Abbey. The author has done a splendid job in putting together their lively recollections with the dry evidence from the records.

It is only when you read the details of the organisation, that the whole scope of the undertaking begins to become clear. There were the inevitable discussions, even arguments, about the principal structure of the great service, but the attention to the details of the preparation of the Abbey is just as intriguing.

I very much doubt whether any two people who attended the Coronation have identical memories of the occasion. Much of that day certainly remains rather a blur in my memory, although I have the most vivid memories of individual incidents. Reading this book brought back many of the half-forgotten recollections of what must have been one of the greatest ceremonies the Abbey has ever witnessed.

Contents

CHAPTER 1

The 'New Elizabethan Age'

SOME TIME IN THE EARLY MORNING OF 6 FEBRUARY 1952 King George VI died in his sleep at Sandringham House – his country residence in Norfolk. At that instant his daughter Princess Elizabeth became Queen. But the new Queen knew nothing of it, for she was 3,000 miles away in Kenya, in a wildlife observation hide built into the branches of a giant fig tree, watching a variety of wild animals that had come to a watering hole to drink. It was to be several hours before her Private Secretary, Martin Charteris, having heard the news from a local reporter, obtained confirmation from London and broke the news to The Queen's husband, the Duke of Edinburgh, who, in turn, told the new Queen that her father had died.

For several weeks concern for the young Queen and the responsibilities that she now faced was overshadowed by sorrow at the loss of a great King who had provided a shining example of service. After the King's funeral, attention focused on arrangements for The Queen's Coronation. In the eyes of many, still experiencing the austerity that followed the Second World War, the event seemed to herald a 'New Elizabethan Age' – an echo, perhaps, of the optimism felt when Elizabeth I came to the Throne in 1558.

To allow time for the arrangements to be made and for Westminster Abbey to be prepared, 2 June 1953 was chosen as Coronation Day – nearly eighteen months after Elizabeth became Queen. A summer Coronation was expected to ensure good weather for the millions who would be celebrating. Although it turned out to be very wet, and the coldest June day for years, the inclement weather did not dampen the enthusiasm of the millions who turned out to cheer The Queen. The interest in this extraordinary and glorious event was genuinely worldwide. Coronations throughout the ages have always affected people in this way, bringing them together in celebration and signalling a new beginning. They are also spectacular events. It was Horace Walpole, after the Coronation of George III in 1761, who wrote to a friend, 'What is the finest sight in the world? A Coronation.'

PREVIOUS PAGE:
A commissioned portrait of The Queen in Coronation robes, painted by Sir Herbert James Gunn from 1953 to 1954.

OPPOSITE PAGE:
Official portrait of the young Princess taken in 1951 by Yousuf Karsh.

The Coronation service has very ancient roots, and the rite has remained basically unchanged for a thousand years since King Edgar was crowned in 973. The structure of the ceremony is based largely on chronicles and ancient liturgical texts which have been adapted through the centuries to suit contemporary political realities. The service consists of six parts:

⚭ The Recognition, during which the people acclaim their new sovereign;

⚭ The Oath, by which the sovereign pledges to serve the people;

⚭ The Anointing with oil on hands, breast and head by the Archbishop of Canterbury, effectively an act of consecration which sets the sovereign apart from the people;

⚭ The Investiture, when the sovereign is presented with the symbols of sovereignty – culminating in the Crown;

⚭ The Homage, when the Church and aristocracy pledge their loyalty;

⚭ The Communion, during which the sovereign receives the sacramental bread and wine in a re-enactment of Christ's last supper.

The new Queen returns to London after her visit to Kenya was cut short by the death of her father.

This order of proceeding was meticulously laid down in the fourteenth-century *Liber Regalis*, one of the Abbey Library's greatest treasures, and has been followed at all Coronations since. Over the centuries the emphasis of the service has swung between sacred and secular. In medieval times the Coronation was primarily a religious rite and a demonstration of political power. By 1821 and the Coronation of George IV its religious significance had been eclipsed by unsurpassed extravagance, which so disgusted the King's successor, William IV, that he did not want a Coronation at all and had to be persuaded. Queen Victoria's Coronation in 1838 was a shambles, with no rehearsal and incompetent clergy making numerous mistakes. In 1902 the Coronation of Edward VII had

Queen Elizabeth II,
Queen Mary and
The Queen Mother wait
at Westminster Hall on
11 February 1952 for
King George VI's coffin
to arrive for the lying
in state.

to be postponed at the last minute, following his emergency operation for appendicitis. By the time it took place, three months later, many of the foreign dignitaries had gone home, and the service had to be curtailed to avoid taxing the King's health. There was no sermon, and the music was reduced. It was even suggested that the Anointing could be reduced to just his hands, rather than hands, head and breast. The King refused: 'If I am going to be done, I am going to be done properly.' For the Coronation of George V the sermon returned, but this was dropped at the ceremonies of both George VI and Elizabeth II.

Deciding on the detailed liturgy for The Queen's Coronation was the responsibility of the Archbishop of Canterbury, Dr Geoffrey Fisher, with help from an advisory committee that included the Dean of Westminster, Dr Alan Don. The non-liturgical arrangements were in the hands of the Earl Marshal, Bernard Fitzalan-Howard, Duke of Norfolk, England's premier peer, helped by Garter King of Arms, Sir George Bellew, the senior herald from the College of Arms – an organisation of ancient foundation whose prime purpose is to maintain a register of pedigrees and arms and to grant new coats of arms to deserving applicants. In charge of the state budget for the event was the Minister of Works, David Eccles. Unlike the Coronation of George VI, for which the budget was not restricted, The Queen's Coronation was organised against an economic backdrop of continuing post-war thrift. Rationing had recently ended, but money and supplies were tight.

Although the basic outline of the service was preordained, there were sensibilities to accommodate. What role, if any, could be given to The Queen's husband, the Duke of Edinburgh? The Queen wanted him to have a part in the service, but the Coronation Committee of the Privy Council, which was overseeing the arrangements, turned the idea down as being too difficult; however, it did agree that he should have a special prayer of blessing and should take communion alongside The Queen. The Duke himself wanted some features 'relevant to the world today' to be included and suggested that, at the Recognition, when those in the Abbey were asked, effectively, if they would accept The Queen, some reference might be made to the various countries of the Commonwealth present. The Home Secretary, Sir David Maxwell Fyfe, said he preferred the traditional simple wording, which made no mention of specific countries, and objected to any change that would give it a more 'Commonwealth character'. South Africa, in particular, he said, was always suspicious of any action that might suggest the Commonwealth was a 'super-state'. He said the emphasis should be on the separateness of the parts rather than the unity of the whole. The Archbishop also did not want any interference. In the end, the traditional form of words was used: 'Sirs, I here present unto you Queen Elizabeth your undoubted Queen: wherefore all you who are come this day to do your homage and service, are you willing to do the same?'

Then, once the congregation had shouted its approval (the only service in the Abbey when the congregation is encouraged to shout), what was The Queen to do? Should she bow in acknowledgement? The Archbishop suggested a half-curtsey, but Garter King of Arms was horrified: the sovereign should never curtsey to her subjects. The Earl Marshal agreed with the Archbishop, and this gave Garter sleepless nights. Eventually the Archbishop asked The Queen. 'Oh, I think a curtsey,' she said. The Archbishop asked if this was a firm ruling. 'Yes,' said The Queen.

There was also concern about what role, if any, the chief minister of the Church of Scotland, the Moderator of the General Assembly, should play. The Dean, himself a Scot, suggested the Moderator might present the Bible to The Queen, normally the Dean's privilege. The Archbishop saw this as a slippery slope and warned that other religious denominations might also start claiming a role in the ceremony. The Dean won the day by pointing out that there were only two churches that The Queen was pledged to maintain – the

The Coronation of a queen is illustrated in the fourteenth-century *Liber Regalis*, which sets out the ceremonial to be used at a Coronation.

Church of England and the Church of Scotland – so that provided a justification. The Dean was particularly worried that, without such a role, the Scots might start agitating for the Stone of Scone to be returned to Scotland, from where Edward I had captured it in 1296. The Stone was significant for Scotland as it was the seat on which Scottish kings had always been inaugurated. It had only recently been restored to the Abbey after being stolen by young Scottish Nationalists, and it was still a delicate issue.

There were two other areas that prompted a great deal of discussion: the Oath and the Homage. Attempts to change them materially came to nothing as time began to run out. It was decided to leave the Oath virtually unchanged from the wording used in 1937 at the Coronation of The Queen's father, George VI, except for changes made necessary by constitutional developments – for example, 'Ireland', named in the Coronation Oath of George VI, was changed to 'Northern Ireland'. In 1937 it had taken nine months to get Commonwealth countries to agree to the wording of the Oath, and those suggesting major

In 1821 the religious significance of King George IV's Coronation was eclipsed by his unsurpassed extravagance.

Archbishop Geoffrey Fisher decided on the detailed liturgy to be followed at the Coronation, basing it largely on that used at previous Coronations.

amendments in 1953 were warned: 'Any attempt to change it now and the Coronation would be held up until June 1954!'

The Homage was more tricky. As it was a non-religious part of the service, some suggested the Homage should take place elsewhere – possibly at Westminster Hall, close by the Abbey – and perhaps at a later time. The Archbishop of Canterbury ruled this out on the grounds that it would detract from the service in the Abbey. And there was another concern. According to tradition, the Archbishop, representing the Lords spiritual, should make his Homage first, kneeling before The Queen and pledging to be 'faithful and true'. The Archbishop was anxious in case the Duke of Edinburgh, as The Queen's husband, would want to follow the precedent set in 1702 by Prince George of Denmark, Queen Anne's husband, and pledge his Homage first. Had the Duke been simply a royal duke, the Archbishop wrote, 'I should cling to my privilege, but as The Queen's husband I think it is right to give way to him – although theoretically it means Church consenting to rank second to a layman.' He need not have worried: the Duke said he would make no claim. As a result the Archbishop was able to go first, with the Duke following. Then would come the other royal dukes (Gloucester and Kent), followed by the senior representatives of each rank of the peerage, in the order dukes, marquesses, earls, viscounts and barons.

But precedence was a minor matter compared with the wider concern expressed by some about why the peers were doing Homage at all. Since the Parliament Acts of 1911 and 1947, the power of the House of Lords had become very limited. If the Homage was to have any meaning, it should be the power-brokers who should kneel before The Queen: trades union leaders and men of industry perhaps. The historian Edward Carpenter, who was Canon of Westminster at the time (and later to become Dean), pointed out that the traditional intention of the Homage was to ensure that any indigenous pockets of energy or possible revolt were brought together to serve the state and the monarchy. The Homage had a very serious political intention, he said, and at The Queen's Coronation this did not really come across. Then there was the question of whether a representative of the common man should pay Homage, as suggested by Prince Philip. Should the Speaker of the House of Commons be that representative? Or the Prime Minister? Just as with attempts to change the Oath, any decision to extend the list of those paying Homage would have needed the approval of Commonwealth countries, and there was no time to obtain this. The Homage therefore remained virtually unchanged from previous Coronations, and probably represented the last time that aristocratic privilege would play such a role at the Coronation service.

With the liturgy agreed, the Archbishop turned his attention to preparing The Queen for the great day. He produced for her what he called 'A Little Book of Private Devotions in Preparation for Her Majesty's Coronation'. Starting a month before Coronation Day, it contained daily prayers and meditations leading up to the ceremony. For the first day the Archbishop wrote for her: 'The whole of my life is a journey to God. In its course are many lesser journeys undertaken for special purposes in answer to a call from God … Such will be my journey to Westminster … I have not chosen this office for myself; he has appointed me to it, and I go to be consecrated to it by him.'

CHAPTER 2

'Taste, style and imagination' as preparations begin

WHILE DETAILS OF THE LITURGY were being thrashed out, consideration was given to the logistics of the occasion. Twenty thousand troops, many of them from Commonwealth countries, would be needed for the procession and to line the route. Hundreds of thousands of foreign visitors would pour into the capital, putting pressure on hotels, many of which had been destroyed during the war. Twenty-seven miles of seating in stands along the processional route had to be built. There were decorations to provide, flowers, floodlighting and fireworks. It was a massive organisational challenge.

The Earl Marshal took over 14 Belgrave Square, not far from Westminster Abbey, for his offices. The Ministry of Works provided whatever he wanted, although it baulked at his request for a flag bearing his coat of arms to fly above his office porch. The Ministry did, however, agree to provide the flagpole. Although the Earl Marshal was in charge of the arrangements, it was the Minister of Works, David Eccles, who provided the vision. Described by one senior civil servant as 'a man of taste, style and imagination', Eccles made it clear that 'It is our duty to express in colour and design the age we live in and The Queen who is to be crowned'. To help plan the processional route to the Abbey a large-scale model was built and shown off to the press. An aide of the Earl Marshal observed: 'Elderly civil servants treated it like a small boy treats his plasticine table.' Then there was the Abbey itself, which had to be transformed: the seating accommodation had to be increased from a normal 2,100 to nearer 7,500 and an Annexe built at the west end where the processions could assemble.

The nave of the Abbey closed on 1 December 1952, allowing the Christmas services to go ahead uninterrupted in the quire and transepts. Then, on 1 January – five months before Coronation Day – the whole Abbey closed. Preparations at previous Coronations had caused much damage to the monuments and fabric of the Abbey. This time, David Eccles made it clear, 'The transformation of the most historic church in the Commonwealth has to

The Minister of Works, David Eccles (left) had a large-scale model built to help plan the special seating on the processional route.

be carried out with minute care. We must return the Abbey to the Dean exactly as it was when we took over.'

First, the floor was covered with felt and a three-inch thick wooden floor laid down. Then the monuments were wrapped in felt and boarded over, as were the choir stalls, the organ screen which divides the nave from the quire, the high altar and the medieval tombs and seats on either side of the altar. The Abbey had been put into cold storage and was unrecognisable. A railway line was laid from the west door to the foot of the altar steps – an area known as the crossing – with branch lines into the transepts north and south so that the hundreds of tons of steel stanchions, scaffolding and wood could be brought in. Tiers of seating were built on either side of the quire and nave, raked steeply up to just beneath the Gothic arches. Three tiers of seats were built in the transepts for the aristocracy and Members of Parliament, and there was extra seating high up in the triforium, beneath the clerestory windows. In the crossing the floor was raised to the level of the pavement in front of the high altar, forming the Coronation theatre. On that the dais was erected, on which was placed The Queen's Throne.

Several stone monuments to the south of the high altar were removed, so that the royal gallery could be built overlooking the theatre.

To furnish the Abbey, 2,000 peers' chairs were needed – made of oak and beech, these were upholstered in blue velour with gold braiding, each with the royal cipher embroidered on the back – and 5,701 stools for those seated in the nave. The specifications were precise. The padding for the stools and chairs had to be 12 per cent horse mane hair, 12 per cent cow tail hair and 76 per cent North American grey winter hog. In addition, the Ministry commissioned 2,287 yards of carpet, 13,000 yards of grey spun rayon for lining the walkways and hiding the scaffolding structures, 1,620 yards of damask for the frontals and 7,700 yards of braid. Thirteen clocks were provided around the Abbey, electrically linked so they all told the same time. Nothing was left to chance. For those high in the triforium who might be taken ill, twenty-four sling chairs were provided to evacuate them down the narrow spiral stairways, where stretchers were useless. In addition, there were ten medical centres set up in strategic parts of the Abbey, each with an examination couch, a table and chair for the attendant, a deckchair and leg-rest for the patient, a cupboard for medical supplies and a portable washstand and mirror. To revive the thirsty there were fifty-two drinking-water fountains at strategic points, with 20,000 waxed paper cups. A June day might be very hot, and with nearly

The artist Sir Henry Rushbury recorded the building of the Annexe at the west end of the Abbey and the special stands where several thousand people watched the processions.

It took more than six months for the seating capacity in the Abbey to be increased from 2,000 to 7,500.

8,000 people (7,500 guests and 400 Gold Staff Officers, or stewards) in a confined space the atmosphere might become oppressive. So several 36-inch diameter fans were installed in the triforium for ventilation. On the day it was so cold that the fans were needed only for short periods. There was accommodation for the press, radio and television to be arranged. Pressure on the limited number of entrances meant some nave windows became doors, accessed from raised walkways outside. Lavatory accommodation had to be vastly increased. One of the largest items to be made was the carpet for the nave – 118 feet long and 17 feet wide, it weighed 5 tons and was woven in Glasgow, at one of the biggest power looms in the country. At any one time up to 200 tradesmen worked at the Abbey, reminded by notices around the building that they were in a sacred place and asked 'to be reverent in your demeanour and careful of the fabric and monuments'. When the seating was finally ready, 1,000 soldiers were brought in, who for more than two and a half hours tested the seating by sitting and rising and then marking time on all the stands.

The Queen herself was involved in decisions about her Throne and her Chair of Estate – the chair in front of the royal gallery that she occupied when she first entered the Abbey. She inspected the Chair of Estate used by her father and pronounced it 'too sumptuously upholstered for ceremonial duty'. Fully adjustable mock-ups of both Throne and Chair were sent to Buckingham Palace for The Queen to try out, dressed in full Coronation robes, so that she could decide on the most comfortable height, width and depth of each. The Queen stressed they had to be dignified and splendid in appearance and in keeping with the setting – there was to be no Festival-of-Britain-type modernity about the furniture. Both were upholstered in crimson damask. The Queen did not favour the Royal Coat of Arms on the back because, when viewed from a distance, it would be 'undistinguished and undistinguishable'. Instead there was to be the royal cipher, surmounted by a crown. At previous Coronations there had been a footstool in front of the Throne. The Queen wanted her feet planted firmly on the ground, so the footstool was dispensed with and the Throne made five inches lower.

If the furniture was traditional, the Annexe certainly was not. David Eccles had been shown previous pseudo-Gothic Annexes built for earlier Coronations. 'There will be nothing pseudo about this Coronation,' he said. As built, the Annexe was box-like modern. It was more than just an assembly place for the processions: the priceless Regalia, including the Crown, the Sceptre and the Orb, were laid here before the service so they could be borne in procession in front of The Queen. There were retiring rooms for the peers in procession, a robing room for The Queen and another for the Duke of Edinburgh; kitchens provided refreshments before and after the service, and the lavatories were plumbed directly into the

Sculptor James Woodford fashioning the Queen's Beasts – mythical creatures officially described as having 'expressions of ferocious loyalty on their aristocratic faces'.

Westminster sewers. At earlier Coronations precious tapestries and Persian carpets had been lent for the Annexe. Tapestries were offered again this time, but the offers were turned down, as they would not have harmonised with the general scheme. On the outside of the Annexe were nine plaster Queen's Beasts – heraldic animals including the lion of England, the unicorn of Scotland, the falcon of the Plantagenets and the greyhound and dragon of the Tudors – and the glass on the west side was engraved with emblems appropriate to the Coronation.

However, not everything went according to plan. So many embroideries were needed for the furnishings that by the time the Earl Marshal got around to ordering them he found all the specialised embroiderers were engaged on regimental work. As a result, some embroideries were not of the standard required. By tradition, during the Anointing an ornate golden canopy is held over the sovereign to hide the sacred ceremony from all eyes. The Earl Marshal discovered the canopy tended to sag but was told it was too late to get it stiffened.

Apart from preparing the Abbey, the Ministry of Works' responsibilities extended to looking after the official guests. Many had to be fed after the service in nearby halls and houses. The Ministry's documents reveal a familiar and homely touch: one handwritten note inquires plaintively about the supply of tea urns. The documents also reveal that the Ministry had to hire special bedroom furniture for The Queen of Tonga – a large lady who endeared herself to the crowd by riding in an open carriage despite the rain, mopping the rain from her brow with her handkerchief. One potential embarrassment was the shortage of carriages for some of the distinguished visitors who would be in the great processions because, some years earlier, the Royal Mews had sold off a number as being surplus to requirements. The new private owners, including the film producer Alexander Korda, offered to lend them back for the occasion.

With the transformation of the Abbey under way, thoughts turned to how those attending should be dressed. For officers in the armed services full-dress uniforms seemed the obvious answer, but the Admiralty was not keen. None had been made since 1939, it said, and those which existed were likely to be in poor condition. The cost of new ones would be huge, and embroidery skills were in short supply; perhaps full-dress should be limited to those in the processions. The Air Ministry, too, said that full-dress uniforms had become obsolete. The Queen thought otherwise. Everyone in the Abbey was to wear the maximum full-dress uniform to which they were entitled, including pre-war uniforms, although no one was expected to spend a lot of money on buying new ones.

Peers and peeresses who did not own their own robes could hire or borrow them from those not able to attend, or have new ones made. But these were not cheap. An Earl's robe with ermine cost 401 guineas (a guinea was £1.05), equivalent to several thousand pounds in today's money, and his coronet 53 guineas. For peeresses below the rank of countess who did

For the peeresses below the rank of countess who did not own their own robes Norman Hartnell designed new ones – the first major change to a peeress's robes for 250 years.

Norman Hartnell designed the Queen's Coronation dress, made of white satin and embroidered with emblems of her kingdoms at home and overseas.

not possess the traditional robe of state Norman Hartnell designed a new one – the first major change to a peeress's Coronation robe for 250 years. It was of crimson velvet trimmed with miniver (fur), sleeveless but with a cape, also of miniver, having rows or bars of ermine tails to indicate the wearer's rank. The robe had an 18-inch-long train. The Duchess of Devonshire caused something of a sensation by wearing a beautiful ancestral off-the-shoulder Coronation gown, which dramatically contrasted with Hartnell's more conservative design.

The six maids of honour who carried The Queen's train – chosen because they were the daughters of earls, marquesses or dukes – were given identical dresses and floral tiaras designed by Norman Hartnell, their heels being adjusted so that each pair on either side of the train were the same height. One of the maids of honour, Lady Anne Coke (now Lady Glenconner), remembers that the dresses, although beautifully embroidered, had not been lined and were very prickly.

Pages wore black patent leather shoes with red heels. Their full uniform included a black three-cornered hat – although they were advised not to buy one, as hats would not be worn. Michael Anson, one of The Queen Mother's pages, remembers having to wear a suspender belt to keep up the two pairs of stockings that were part of his uniform – a silk pair worn over a cotton pair. The Archbishop's Chaplain, the Revd Canon Eric Jay, was something of a rebel and, according to an anecdote at the time, when told he would have to wear court dress under his cassock, said he intended to wear football shorts.

Dress for civilians not taking part in the procession was evening dress, morning dress or dark lounge suits, while women had to wear evening dress or afternoon dress, with tiaras or a headdress of light veiling. Norman Hartnell designed fifteen types of headdress approved by The Queen and held an exhibition of his designs at his Mayfair salon so that guests could choose. For the Dean and Chapter new blue copes were made, boldly sporting lions and unicorns. One Canon ruefully suggested that, once dressed in them, 'We shall look like the Dean's Beasts.'

Chapter 3

Music fit for a Queen

FROM THE VERY EARLIEST TIMES music has played a vital part in the Coronation service, not least because, before amplification, few in the Abbey would have heard a single word of the service and would have relied on music to indicate where they were in the liturgy. The choice of who should take charge of the music was the Earl Marshal's, and the Dean of Westminster, Alan Don, lobbied hard for the job to be given, as in the three previous Coronations, to the Organist and Master of the Choristers at the Abbey – in 1953, Dr William McKie. The Master of The Queen's Music, Sir Arnold Bax, might have expected the role, but Don stressed to the Earl Marshal that it would be fatal to put him in charge as he was not an organist 'and would not, I think, readily secure the co-operation of church musicians'. McKie was considered ideal, partly because he had impressed everyone with the way he handled the music for The Queen's wedding in 1947. Although he had a volatile personality, he was a superb administrator and was given the job. He convened an advisory committee that included his predecessor Sir Ernest Bullock, Director of Music at the Coronation of George VI, and Sir Arnold Bax.

Some of the music chosen was preordained: Handel's 'Zadok the Priest', written for the Coronation of George II in 1727, was indispensable, and Sir Hubert Parry's 'I Was Glad', as an opening anthem during the monarch's entry procession, had been such a success at the three previous Coronations that it could not be bettered. But clearly it was important that new music be commissioned from some of Britain's leading contemporary composers, and McKie sounded them out. Ralph Vaughan Williams was asked if he would like to compose a new *Te Deum* to be sung at the end of the service, as he had done for the Coronation of George VI. He declined, although he was happy for his *Creed* and *Sanctus* from his Communion service in G minor to be used. He also agreed to write a short unaccompanied anthem to be sung while The Queen received communion. Thus was born the classic motet 'O Taste and See how

Gracious the Lord is', an exquisite miniature still popular with church choirs. It was also the only anthem to contain a 'solo', sung at the Coronation by three Abbey choristers.

Vaughan Williams's other major influence on the music was his suggestion that there should be something for the congregation to sing. McKie's advisory committee was divided. McKie backed the idea, but four of his team were against, including Bullock and John Dykes Bower, Organist of St Paul's Cathedral, who did not think the congregation was of the kind to sing. Dean Don was also concerned. But they were out-flanked when the Archbishop of Canterbury, himself in favour, put it to The Queen, who 'thought well of it'. So Vaughan Williams made a special arrangement of the hymn 'All People that on Earth do Dwell' to the tune of 'The Old Hundredth', with trumpet fanfares. Later McKie and the Archbishop agreed it would have been better with a plain organ accompaniment and no trimmings.

The organ caused concern in the days leading up to the Coronation. It had not been used for several months, and with all the preparations for the service it was full of dust and dirt. It required several days of attention, and during the rehearsals and the service itself there were four organ tuners on standby to deal with any problems.

Australian-born William McKie, Organist and Master of the Choristers at the Abbey, directed the music at the Coronation, for which he was knighted.

George Frederic Handel's 'Zadok the Priest' has been sung at every Coronation since that of George II in 1727.

Ralph Vaughan Williams (right) composed an exquisite miniature anthem, 'O Taste and See', to be sung while the Queen took Communion.

William Walton (far right) wrote a full length *Te Deum*, its syncopated rhythms a contrast with the more traditional music at the service.

Five anthems were included in the printed Order of Service, to be available during the Homage depending on how long it took. McKie decided on the order at the last moment, indicating which was to be sung by having someone hold up a numbered card. The only newly composed anthem in the list was by the Canadian composer Healey Willan – 'O Lord our Governor'. It was of particular significance for Canada that Willan should have his anthem sung, and his friends clubbed together to pay for his journey to London to attend the Coronation. There was time for only two others: the sixteenth-century 'Rejoice in the Lord Always' and S.S. Wesley's 'Thou Wilt Keep Him in Perfect Peace'. McKie resisted the temptation to compose an anthem himself. One of his predecessors at the Abbey, Sir Frederick Bridge, had shown no such modesty and had composed Homage anthems for the Coronations of both Edward VII and George V, neither of which has stood the test of time.

Among the other new choral works composed for the service, Sir William Walton's *Te Deum* was the most impressive. The Archbishop of Canterbury had tried to persuade him to use the shortened form of the *Te Deum*, but Walton insisted on the full version and produced a masterpiece. Its syncopated rhythms were a challenge, and Walton himself came to rehearse the Abbey Choir. Walton attended the Coronation in his Oxford Doctor of Music robes, which included a hat in which he is said to have carried a supply of miniature whisky bottles to sustain him during the service.

The Abbey's choristers were among the 480 musicians in the choir and orchestra who took part in the service.

In addition to the choral works there were three new orchestral pieces, one of which was Walton's 'Orb and Sceptre'. Sir Arthur Bliss composed a 'Processional', and Sir Arnold Bax produced a 'Coronation March', which was due to be played immediately after the National Anthem at the end of the service. At the final rehearsal the Earl Marshal was not happy about it, saying it felt 'a bit thin'. So Elgar's magnificent 'Pomp and Circumstance March No. 1' was played instead, with the Bax march following it.

Benjamin Britten was asked to write an orchestral piece, to be played before the Abbey service. He was already writing a Coronation opera (*Gloriana*) but agreed to do so if he possibly could. Unfortunately four months before the Coronation he fell ill with flu, and then flooding in Aldeburgh, where he lived, caused more disruption and he finally had to refuse.

Apart from deciding on the music, McKie had also to decide who should be in the choir and orchestra, totalling more than 480 people. The full choirs of Westminster Abbey, St Paul's Cathedral, the Chapel Royal and St George's Chapel, Windsor, took part, as well as representatives from other choirs, including those of several cathedrals and colleges – a total of 182 trebles, 37 altos, 62 tenors and 67 basses. As in 1937, there were representatives from Australia, New Zealand, South Africa and Canada. Had anyone asked why singers from other countries were not included, they would have been told that it was not meant to be an 'Empire' choir and had to be limited to singers used to this kind of music. Surprisingly, although there were nineteen female singers from the Dominions, there were none from Britain, which upset British sopranos and contraltos.

Seating for the choir was very cramped. McKie discovered that one row of boys, seated in the front row just behind the organ casing, could not stand properly and could not see or be heard. McKie had laid down an edict that any choir member missing one of the full choir rehearsals would not be allowed to sing at the service. Unfortunately two of Britain's leading musicians, Boris Ord, Director of Music at King's College, Cambridge, and the countertenor Alfred Deller, were booked to appear at a Festival Hall concert and could not attend one of the rehearsals. Despite urgent pleading, McKie disqualified them, saying that there could be no exceptions. The seating for the choir was above the north and south quire aisles, where many singers could not see McKie. His beat was relayed by sub-conductors, a system that worked well. The orchestra was made up of leading players from various orchestras and, despite having relatively little rehearsal together, they acquitted themselves brilliantly. The music was a triumph, and William McKie was knighted in the Coronation Honours.

The organ needed a thorough clean before the Coronation because of thick dust caused by preparations for the ceremony.

CHAPTER 4

Practice makes (almost) perfect

MANY FUNCTIONS AT A CORONATION are traditionally performed by holders of certain offices, by descendants of ancient families, or more frequently by certain landowners. Those wanting to stake their claim have to make their case before the Court of Claims, specially constituted for each Coronation and consisting of members of the Privy Council's Coronation Committee. For The Queen's Coronation the Court considered twenty-one claims, including one from the Dean and Chapter of Westminster to instruct The Queen in the Coronation rites and ceremonies, to which the Court agreed. The Dean and Chapter's formal claim also set out what traditionally they had a right to receive. It included 'six yards of sarcenet [a soft silk cloth], The Queen's upper vestments in which she comes into the church, the stage, Throne, royal seats, tapestries, chairs, cushions, carpets, cloths and all the ornaments with which the stage and the church shall be embellished'. The Dean and Chapter can hardly have expected the Court to acquiesce. In previous Coronations they had received a sum of money in lieu, which they had accepted without prejudice. It was to be the same this time.

The Court considered the other claims and approved most of them. One it rejected was a claim on behalf of the Duke of Newcastle, the Lord of the Manor of Worksop in Nottinghamshire, 'to present The Queen with a glove for her right hand, and for a deputy to support Her Majesty's arm while holding the Royal Sceptre'. It was rejected on the grounds that the Duke had merged his estates in a limited company, and the Court ruled that such rights could not be vested in a company. The glove was presented instead by Lord Woolton, who was appointed to the role by The Queen.

Deciding who should be in the 7,500-strong congregation presented a major headache, as many would expect to attend and many more would want to. There was seating, for example, for Members of Parliament and their wives, but not all the House of Lords could

The Coronation stretched the BBC's outside broadcast resources to the limit, but its coverage proved a worldwide success heralding a new era in broadcasting.

be accommodated. There was talk of a ballot, but some preferred to sit in the stands outside the Abbey, where they could have their family with them and follow the service broadcast on loudspeakers. Then there were representatives from all walks of life, from local communities, professional and voluntary organisations and charities, foreign diplomats and visiting royalty. Fifty-one places were allotted to religious bodies, although, as in recent Coronations, the small allocation of seats to the Roman Catholic Church was declined. The Dean and Chapter were dismayed to find that the forty-five seats allocated for their families and friends (fewer than at previous Coronations) were not, as in earlier times, in one block in the muniment room, from where they had a good chance of a view of sorts, but scattered around the Abbey. One peer was not sure if he would be allowed to attend, as he was divorced. The Earl Marshal reassured him, 'This is a Coronation, not Ascot.' (Divorcees were not allowed in the Royal Enclosure at the annual Royal Ascot race meeting.)

Many previous Coronations had been badly organised, but this time the Earl Marshal realised there would be no room for mistakes, and nothing was left to chance. Having directed the Coronation of George VI – at the tender age of twenty-nine – he was aware of the pitfalls and so was well prepared. Rehearsals of all aspects of the ceremony were arranged, including a spectacular final dress rehearsal witnessed by more than 1,100 invited guests and 350 members of the press, with the Duchess of Norfolk standing in for The Queen.

The Coronation had to be perfect for one very good reason: television cameras were to be allowed in. The BBC had won a hard-fought battle against the forces of conservatism. Initially, the Duke of Norfolk and the Archbishop of Canterbury recommended that television should be banned or, if allowed at all, should be confined to the processions west of the organ screen, 'but we shall begin by resisting television altogether'. What if The Queen made a mistake? It would be instantly transmitted and could not be rectified, they argued. There was concern that television would have a 'disintegrating' effect, allowing people to watch in the privacy of their homes rather than, as they should be, united in churches throughout the land, attending great civic services together. The Dean of Westminster was not happy about the bright lights needed for television, especially if it was a hot day; the consequences might be disastrous, and the glare would distress those in the upper stands. It would also remove all sense of mystery from the Abbey, leaving it 'blatant and vulgarised'. The Queen herself was said not to want the service televised, and the Cabinet agreed.

But there were powerful arguments in favour. At the previous Coronation filming had been allowed, and the Duke and the Archbishop realised that, if the lighting required for television was no greater than that needed for colour filming, it would be difficult to justify keeping TV cameras out. They did point out, however, that a film could be censored before release. After the Coronation of George VI the then Archbishop and Earl Marshal had viewed the completed film at midnight and were able to cut out the Communion service as well as other parts considered unsuitable – including shots of Queen Mary crying – before it was distributed. Officials expressed concern that, while people would watch the Communion service on television in all kinds of uncontrolled groups and gatherings, a film was different because it would be watched by people in the dark in a cinema, with everyone concentrating in conditions 'favourable to reverent reception'. The Prime Minister, Winston Churchill, said he found this distinction 'too subtle' for him. The Archbishop wrote later that from the first word it was obvious that Churchill had made up his mind that everything should be televised, except perhaps the Anointing and the Communion. The Archbishop realised that Churchill was alarmed at what the public reaction would be if television were banned, and the Archbishop himself admitted he could see no logic in keeping the non-religious aspects of the ceremony – the secular pomp and the Crowning – away from television. Lighting tests showed that television actually needed less powerful lighting than colour filming, as the Head of Religious Broadcasting at the BBC had assured them. The Queen quickly changed her mind, and eventually it was agreed that the service could be televised except for the Communion, and provided the Anointing was only seen at long distance and from the west. The BBC had won the day.

Once the broadcasting of the ceremony was agreed, special arrangements had to be made so that the sound could be picked up. A small hole was made in the carpet under The Queen's Throne, through which a microphone lead was fed so that the Homage could be heard. The

The gold Ampulla contains the holy oil for anointing the sovereign and was probably first used at Henry IV's Coronation in 1399.

The twelfth-century gold anointing spoon, into which the holy oil is poured, is the oldest surviving piece of Coronation regalia.

microphone itself was attached to the leg of the Throne and gilded for disguise. Similarly a microphone was fixed to the kneeling stool at the Chair of Estate; when the kneeling stool was removed during the ceremony, the wire was cut with wire cutters. A microphone was even strapped to the top of the Coronation Chair. One of the five cameras in the Abbey was placed in the organ loft, in a very tight space close to the conductor. Floorboards were removed to make room for the feet of the very small cameraman, 'whose back was menaced by a ring of steel-sharp cello pegs' and whose head was several times struck by the conductor's baton.

The Ministry of Works had agreed to hand over the completed Abbey to the Earl Marshal by 1 June – the day before the Coronation – but it had not foreseen the need for rehearsals. It was much put out by demands that everything should be ready a week or so before, with everything in place and the carpets laid.

Individual parts of the service were rehearsed separately. The Queen herself rehearsed at Buckingham Palace, where a floor plan had been marked out, but later attended several rehearsals in the Abbey in secret. The fact that screens had been erected so that those working in the Abbey could not see her did not stop journalists waiting outside offering workmen £50 to reveal what had gone on. So secret were her attendances that, at one afternoon rehearsal, the Earl Marshal at the last minute realised he had forgotten to inform the two supporting bishops who stood on either side of The Queen: the Bishop of Durham and the Bishop of Bath and Wells. An emergency call was put out for them. As a result, an express train had to make an unscheduled stop at Bath to allow the Bishop of Bath and Wells to board. He arrived at Paddington and was taken by police car to the Abbey, where he arrived twenty minutes late. Meanwhile Michael Ramsey, Bishop of Durham (and later to be Archbishop of Canterbury), arrived by police car from Cambridge just ten minutes late. He greeted The Queen by apologising for being late, saying he had been 'arrested' in Cambridge having a haircut.

Once The Queen had arrived at the Coronation theatre at the start of the service, she was to make a genuflection to the altar, along with her maids of honour, and this took some practice to get right. Another concern was whether the St Edward's Crown, with which she was to be crowned, would be uncomfortably heavy for her to wear during the rest of the ceremony – it weighed nearly 5 pounds. Queen Victoria and Edward VII had been crowned with the much lighter Imperial State Crown, weighing just over 2 pounds, and George V wore the St Edward's Crown for barely four minutes before exchanging it for the lighter crown. The Queen opted for the St Edward's Crown, taking it off to receive Communion before replacing it, and only finally exchanging it for the Imperial State Crown during the Recess and the procession from the Abbey. The Queen enjoyed the rehearsals, comparing them to a family party rather than rehearsals for a great state occasion, and she certainly impressed the Archbishop. He wrote: 'Throughout the whole of the rehearsal The Queen was at her absolute best – sincere, gay, happy, intensely interested, asking all the right questions about her movements and carrying them out very naturally and impressively.'

At the first full rehearsal, on 27 May, the Earl Marshal was less than pleased with the pages, whose job it was to carry their masters' coronets in procession and hand them over just before the Crowning so that they could all put them on at the same time.

The Imperial Mantle, made of cloth-of-gold for George IV's Coronation in 1821, is embroidered with emblems of the United Kingdom.

He told them all to get their hair cut and even threatened to summon their headmasters by telegram, a threat which, of course, he had no intention of carrying out. Philip Gurdon (now Lord Cranworth), page to Lord Hastings, remembers the Earl Marshal telling him, 'You will be behind Lord Hastings, and you know that the further back in the procession you are the grander you are, so you are grander than Lord Hastings, but not as grand as The Queen.'

Throughout there was tension between the Archbishop and Garter King of Arms. According to the Archbishop, 'Garter and I fought frequently, always ending up on very friendly terms. If he told me I did not know how to run a show, I told him he knew nothing about ceremonial in an ecclesiastical setting.'

The Earl Marshal's final full rehearsal, on 29 May, was not without incident. One of the officials of the College of Arms – or Heralds, as they are called – Lord Lyon King of Arms, fainted. Dressed in his heraldic tabard, he came down with a terrific thud, which was picked up by a nearby microphone. According to one of the Gold Staff Officers close by, he looked like a court card lying on the gold carpet. By Coronation Day he was back to his normal self. The MP Tom Driberg, who had watched the final rehearsal, said that The Queen's maids of honour, who carried her train, looked too pale in the strong artificial light and suggested that they should be made up with more of a suntan. He was not impressed with the Archbishop's singing, and he criticised the Lord Chancellor for being restless. There was also a problem

St Edward's Crown, like most of the regalia, dates from 1661. It weighs 5 lbs (2.23 kg) and is used for the Crowning ceremony.

with the hymn: two of the verses were to be sung by the choir alone, but there was no indication of this in the printed non-musical edition of the Order of Service that many were given.

As The Queen was crowned, the peers and peeresses had to put on their coronets and shout, 'God Save The Queen, Long Live The Queen, God Save The Queen.' Unfortunately the shouts were coming too late. The Earl Marshal stressed they had to learn to put on their coronets and shout at the same time. Others observed that the Lord Chancellor looked very odd as he tried to wear his coronet without the wig for which it was designed, with the result that it sat on the bridge of his nose.

Sitting in the triforium were the forty academic scholars known as Queen's Scholars, from Westminster School, one of Britain's best-known independent schools. By tradition they have the right to welcome the sovereign as he or she emerges from under the screen into the quire in the entry procession, by singing, in this case, *Vivat Regina Elizabetha*. In earlier centuries they shouted their exhortation at random moments during the ceremony. Their enthusiasm was tamed for the Coronation of Edward VII, when the words were incorporated into Parry's opening anthem, 'I Was Glad'. One of them, Gavin Ross, remembers the difficulty they had with some of the boys, who, not being musicians, found the *Vivats* tricky. 'They were quite high-pitched, and we were singing them with no orchestral accompaniment. If we had gone flat it would have shown up dreadfully when the orchestra came in again, but we weren't too bad.' They had been rehearsing their contribution for weeks, but at the last rehearsal it was noted that they would have to sing louder.

After the final rehearsal the Earl Marshal issued his verdict: he said that the Homage had given rise to some concerns, Lord Salisbury needed help to get up after kneeling and Lord Mowbray needed 'tuning up'. After the Anointing, he advised the Archbishop not to rub the oil off so violently. And he wanted less talking and moving about when getting ready for the procession out of the Abbey. In general, though, the rehearsals had gone well. Now there were three clear days of relaxation before the day itself.

The Royal Sceptre, representing the monarch's power under God, is set with the largest cut diamond in the world, the First Star of Africa weighing 530 carats.

The Imperial State Crown was worn by the Queen as she left the Abbey for her procession to Buckingham Palace and is used each year at the State Opening of Parliament.

CHAPTER 5

Coronation Day

AT THE ABBEY, CORONATION DAY began at 4.00 a.m., when the 400 Gold Staff Officers, or stewards – mostly senior officers from the three armed services – arrived for breakfast in a marquee in Dean's Yard. In an ancient room known as the Jericho Parlour, just off the nave of the Abbey, the Yeoman Warders of the Tower, or 'Beefeaters', roused themselves. Eight of them had arrived from the Tower of London the night before with the Regalia, which had been placed on tables in the adjacent Jerusalem Chamber. In pairs, each man armed with a revolver and twelve rounds of ammunition, they had taken it in turns to guard the precious objects while their colleagues slept on mattresses on the floor.

At 5.30 a.m. the Gold Staff Officers synchronised their watches by Big Ben and were given a last-minute briefing. In particular, they were told to make sure they did not block the view of any guest, although some were later to be accused of having done just that. They were given a picnic lunch to take with them and left for their positions in the Abbey before the doors opened to guests at 6.00 a.m. Despite assurances from the Ministry of Works, they found that not all was in order: all the lavatories were found to be locked, and someone had taken all the paper. In the Coronation theatre an unexpected guest was found asleep on the soft cushion of the Coronation Chair – Matins, a cat belonging to one of the Minor Canons and a frequent visitor to the Abbey during the preparations.

Meanwhile, some miles away in Mayfair, the Duke and Duchess of Devonshire were setting out for the Abbey in their family carriage, together with their young son the nine-year-old Marquess of Hartington (now the Duke). He was page to the Duke's mother, the Dowager Duchess, who was Mistress of the Robes. Pages were meant to be between the ages of twelve and fifteen, but an exception was made in his case because of his particular family connections. He recalls that it was his father's decision to use the family carriage. They had recruited a local drayman as coachman and used some local horses to pull it. 'St James's Street

Attended by her maids of honour, The Queen arrives at the Abbey for her Coronation.

is steeper than it looks, and as we came down with the coachman keeping the horses to a trot, we were overtaken by the Marquess of Bath in his coach at a canter.' The two carriages arrived on the Mall just as the thousands of people who had camped out all night were stirring themselves. 'Those were rather austere days and Dukes in carriages were not necessarily what people approved of, so there was some slightly sarcastic cheering.' Then, to the Duke's annoyance, the coachman got lost.

He was a Derbyshire man and did not know the London streets. Being inside the coach, we could not communicate with him and my father was getting more and more upset as he hated being late for anything and to be late for the Coronation was unacceptable, though in fact there was plenty of time.

Shortly after eight o'clock a motor coach drove down the Mall with choristers from the Chapel Royal on board, dressed in their colourful seventeenth-century uniforms. The cheering for them was more enthusiastic.

When the Duke's carriage did finally arrive at the Abbey, there was more trouble in store. 'As my father was getting out of the coach my sword caught in his robes and ripped them. There was a piece about 18 inches long hanging down. Actually, he was not as angry with me as he might have been.' The Earl Marshal had anticipated this sort of problem, and there were tailors in the Annexe to effect running repairs.

Although the Coronation service was not due to start for several hours, guests were queuing to get in as soon as the doors opened. Security was tight, but at least one person managed to gain access without a ticket. She was a member of the Abbey Choir School's teaching staff who accompanied a ticketed colleague taking in several of the junior probationary choirboys, also with tickets, who were to sit in the triforium. With the tickets bunched together and uncounted, the policeman on the cloister door waved them all through.

The doors finally closed to invited guests at 8.30 a.m. With the service not due to start until 11.15 a.m., everyone was in for a long wait – but there was plenty to see as the formal processions began. Some peeresses only just made it to their seats in time before the processions started, as many wanted to walk up the aisle on their own and not alongside others to show themselves off and be seen by all.

The Dean's first duty on Coronation morning had been to fill the Ampulla with the oil for the Anointing, which was kept in his safe. With the job safely completed, at 9.30 a.m. a procession set off from the Jerusalem Chamber with members of the Abbey clergy carrying the Regalia, which included the Ampulla, Sceptre and Orb, with the Dean carrying St Edward's Crown. They made their way through the cloisters, led by the Abbey Choir and The Queen's Scholars, into the Abbey. When they reached the Coronation theatre, the Regalia were placed on the altar, except for the Ampulla and the Imperial State Crown, which were taken into St Edward's Chapel, where the oil was consecrated by the Bishop of Gloucester, Dr Clifford Woodward, a former Canon of Westminster. Leaving the Ampulla and Crown in the Chapel, the clergy re-

The Queen, flanked by the Bishop of Durham (on her right) and the Bishop of Bath and Wells, reaches the Coronation theatre for the start of the service.

emerged and carried the rest of the Regalia in procession to the Annexe, where they were placed on an altar-like table ready for The Queen's entry procession. Ironically, here they were at their most vulnerable, especially to inquisitive fingers. One of the pages, Henry (now Sir Henry) Keswick, page to Lord Alanbrooke, remembers: 'I had been told there were two drop pearls on the top of St Edward's Crown which had been worn by Queen Elizabeth I, and I remember holding them in my hands, each between a thumb and forefinger. I could have put the Crown on if I had wanted to – it was just sitting there.'

At 10.00 a.m. the Archbishop of Canterbury arrived in the Annexe, confident that all would go well. Two days earlier he had gone to the Palace to see The Queen and the Duke of Edinburgh, to pray with them and give them his blessing. At the same time he took the opportunity to ask The Queen to sign his copy of the Queen's 'Book of Private Devotions'. By now the Annexe was full, and there was not enough room for everyone to sit down to wait.

As the service began The Queen sat in her Chair of Estate, with her family in the royal gallery behind her.

Lord Hastings, who was quite elderly and was to carry one of the items of the Regalia in the procession, had attended the previous Coronation and knew the ropes. According to his page, Philip Gurdon (now Lord Cranworth), 'He had brought his little campstool with him. The press were thrilled with that. I remember him sitting down on it in the Annexe with his robes round him like a tent.' Field Marshal Viscount Montgomery did manage to find a seat and was seen reading *The Times* account of the conquest of Everest by a team of British mountaineers. The Duchess of Gloucester ticked off the young Prince William of Gloucester for walking informally with his hands behind his back. Another page was seen polishing his master's coronet with his sleeve 'as though he was the opening bowler keeping the shine on the ball', according to a reporter.

Many of those waiting had brought a picnic, but even so there was pressure on the coffee room. One of the pages, John (now Sir John) Aird, wrote in his schoolboy diary, 'the Clergy barged in first, soon followed by the peers and pages'. Michael Anson, one of The Queen Mother's pages, remembers that the Bishop of Durham, Michael Ramsey, had brought his refreshments concealed in his mitre. 'He took it off, proffered it to us and said, "Have a sandwich".'

The Archbishop was particularly impressed with the way the Scots Guards who were lining the walls round the Annexe presented arms. 'First one group of three or four, then the next little group and so on rippling round the room without a single word being spoken.' Field Marshal Montgomery, who was to carry the Royal Standard, told him it was not a procedure in the book, 'but it is done like that to avoid anyone having to give a word of command to the whole lot'.

Of The Queen's six maids of honour, two followed her in the coach to help her dismount, while the other four waited for her in the Annexe. One, Lady Jane Heathcote-Drummond-Willoughby (now Baroness Willoughby de Eresby), arrived to find her father, who was also in the procession, shivering in his robes because it was so cold.

I got him a cup of coffee. He had a bad leg from the War and did not want to queue. We were spoiled because we were allowed to sit in the Duke of Edinburgh's robing room. Someone had brought a radio and we listened to the procession approaching the Abbey. Just before The Queen arrived we were all moved out again.

Adhering to a strict timetable, processions from the Annexe into the Abbey set out at regular intervals, taking groups of guests to their places: first the junior members of the Royal Family, followed by the royal and other representatives of foreign states, the procession of the rulers of states under Her Majesty's protection (including Queen Salote of Tonga), the Dean and Canons of Westminster, the procession of the 'Princes and Princesses of the Blood Royal' and finally the procession of Queen Elizabeth The Queen Mother and Princess Margaret.

At 10.36 a.m., anticipating the start of the service, the congregation stood up in hushed silence thinking that The Queen was about to appear, when, from several parts of the Abbey, cleaners emerged armed with carpet sweepers to restore the scuffed carpet to its pristine state. The tension broke, and everyone laughed and sat down again to await the real start. The congregation may have been amused, but the Archbishop certainly was not: 'The presence of cleaners at this stage, after the many solemn processions finishing with that of The Queen Mother, created an undesirable and disturbing anticlimax', he wrote.

Finally, at 11.00 a.m., The Queen arrived in the Annexe looking rather nervous, the cheers of the crowds giving warning of her arrival. There was a slight delay as the Royal Dukes prepared themselves and the procession lined up. Lord Cranworth remembers how impressed he was with the Earl Marshal.

In a simple white robe The Queen waits while the golden canopy is held over her for the Anointing.

He was totally in charge. I imagined he would have the equivalent of civil servants organising it for him, but no, he seemed to do it all. I don't think he had a clipboard, but he was absolutely on the ball. He certainly came and told us where we had to stand and what we had to do.

With The Queen's procession about to start, Michael Willoughby, the Senior Queen's Scholar, perched in the triforium with a good view of the west door, waved a handkerchief to cue the organ to start playing. Just before The Queen moved, she turned round to her maids of honour and said, 'Ready, girls?' There was a fanfare, and they were off. The processional anthem was Parry's 'I Was Glad', and the conductor, William McKie, said later that as soon as that got under way he knew everything would go well.

The Queen's procession up the nave was not as slow as it should have been. The *Vivats* from The Queen's Scholars should have greeted The Queen as she entered the quire from under the organ screen. In fact, she had already reached the steps up to the Coronation theatre when they rang out. The Queen's Scholars were not the only ones to sing the *Vivats*. Sitting opposite them in the south triforium were about forty non-scholars from Westminster School, known as 'town boys'. Some of them joined in – perhaps so they could claim to their descendants that they too had sung at The Queen's Coronation. Baroness Willoughby de Eresby was particularly moved by the music. 'I suppose for the first time I was aware of the power of music. It just carried you through. Visually, though, it was all rather a blur because of the strong television lights bearing down.' Her pair on the opposite side of the train, now Lady Glenconner, was equally struck by the splendour of it all: 'It was like being in a medieval pageant.'

As The Queen entered the Coronation theatre for the first time, she and her maids of honour should have made their carefully rehearsed curtsey to the altar – but she forgot, and neither of the supporting bishops dared remind her. To those in the congregation, though, the slip-up went unnoticed.

As The Queen stood by the Coronation Chair, the Archbishop went to the four sides of the theatre: 'Sirs, I here present unto you Queen Elizabeth, your undoubted Queen: Wherefore all you who are come this day to do your homage and service, are you willing to do the same?'

The congregation shouted in reply, 'God save Queen Elizabeth.' Then came the Oath when The Queen promised to govern her peoples 'according to their respective laws and customs', to cause law and justice, in mercy, to be executed in all her judgements, to maintain the laws of God and the true profession of the Gospel and to maintain 'the Protestant Reformed Religion established by law'. The Moderator of the General Assembly of the Church of Scotland presented the Bible to The Queen, as the Archbishop said, 'to keep your Majesty ever mindful of the Law and the Gospel of God', to which the Moderator added the words, 'Here is Wisdom; This is the royal Law; These are the lively Oracles of God.' Oxford University Press, which had printed the Bible, had been anxious that the colour of the binding should not clash with the colour of the cope of the Bishop who was to carry it in the entry procession. They were reassured a red binding would be fine. At the previous Coronation the Bible had been produced by Cambridge University Press, but it was so big that no bishop could carry it in procession, and they had to produce a smaller one instead.

Then began the Communion service with an anthem, the reading of the Epistle and the Gospel and the singing of the Creed. Next came the most sacred part of the service, the Anointing, beginning with the singing of the 'Veni Creator Spiritus' and Handel's 'Zadok the Priest'. During this anthem The Queen took off her crimson robe, with its long train, and put on instead an unadorned full-skirted white robe, which, rather like a hospital robe, fastened down the back. Lady Glenconner remembers it was the job of the Lord Great Chamberlain, the Marquess of Cholmondeley, to do up the fastenings, 'but he had clearly never had to do anything like this before and at the rehearsal had been all fingers and thumbs dealing with the hooks and eyes, prompting the Earl Marshal to have them changed to poppers.'

Now, as The Queen sat in the Coronation Chair, four Knights of the Garter brought the golden canopy to hold over her, to keep her hidden from all eyes. Unfortunately the solemn effect was somewhat disturbed as the canopy dragged against the microphone fastened to the top of the Chair and an unpleasant rasping noise was heard through the church. As at the rehearsal, despite the Knights' best efforts, the canopy sagged.

The Dean poured some oil from the Ampulla into the Anointing Spoon and held it out for the Archbishop to dip his thumb in it. The oil had been specially made to a traditional formula said to date from the time of the Coronation of Charles II in 1661, which included sesame, alcohol and olive oil, highly perfumed with additions including jasmine, cinnamon, musk, civet and ambergris. A large amount had been made for the Coronation of Edward VII and then also used at the Coronations of George V and George VI. The remainder, kept in the deanery at the Abbey, was destroyed during the Second World War, when much of the deanery was burnt out, so a new batch had been made.

The Archbishop of Canterbury raises St Edward's Crown aloft moments before crowning The Queen at the climax of the service.

The Archbishop first anointed The Queen's hands, and then, as he wrote later, he stepped back and dipped his thumb again to anoint The Queen's breast and head. Unfortunately, by the time he had said the prescribed prayer, the oil on his thumb had evaporated. Nevertheless, he pressed his thumb on The Queen's breast and head 'which was all that was necessary', and then wiped her two hands clean.

The Queen knelt for a blessing and was then arrayed in the traditional robes of sovereignty – the *Colobium Sindonis* (literally, 'the little gown of linen') and the *Supertunica* of cloth of gold. Sitting once again in the Coronation Chair, she was presented with the spurs, which she touched and returned, followed by the sword, with which The Queen was urged to 'do justice, stop the growth of iniquity, protect the holy Church of God, help and defend widows and orphans, restore the things that are gone to decay, maintain the things that are restored, punish and reform what is amiss, and confirm what is in good order'.

The Queen took the sword and delivered it to the altar. Now it was the Archbishop's turn to make a mistake. As The Queen resumed her seat, the Archbishop stepped forward ready to take the Armills, or Bracelets, from the Dean. The Dean did not appear, however, and there was a long pause. The Archbishop suddenly remembered he should have waited until a peer had collected the Sword from the altar. He threw up his hands in annoyance at what he had done and retreated. The Queen noticed his mistake and told him afterwards that she had done her best to stop him coming out and was willing him not to. The Archbishop wrote later, 'I said that in that case we were all square. She had failed to will me at this point and I had failed to will her to curtsey.' Garter also noticed the Archbishop's mistake and with mischievous glee told him later that he liked 'the charming little blessing you gave The Queen' at that point in the service.

Next, The Queen was invested with the symbols of sovereignty – the Armills, or Bracelets, the Royal Robe with the Stole Royal, the Orb, the Ring, the Sceptre and the Rod with the Dove. There had been much discussion over the reintroduction of the Armills into the service. Indeed there had been confusion over what exactly they were. In the past some had thought the Armills referred to the royal stole worn around the neck, which was then tied to the monarch's arms. Now, though, it was clear the word meant 'Bracelets'. Garter had been worried that people might associate the Bracelets with handcuffs or, as he ponderously put it 'with implements of restraint now used daily by servants of the law and therefore closely associated with a side of life to which, though it is ever with us, it is undesirable to draw undue attention'. Reintroducing them might be considered unlucky, he thought, although he added quickly that he himself was not superstitious. Although there was an ancient pair among the Crown Jewels, he suggested that new ones should be made of gold contributed by Commonwealth countries. Bracelets had not been used at a Coronation service since the sixteenth century; 'thus the new Bracelets would acquire a suitable symbolic meaning as representing the bond between the sovereign and all her people'. Garter's idea was taken up, and though it had been too late for the various countries to contribute individual gifts of gold, the cost of the Bracelets was shared between them. In the Archbishop's 'Book of Private Devotions', which The Queen had studied, he had suggested she should think: 'As I receive them I declare my willing acceptance of His restraining hand upon my wrist, His yoke upon my neck, the robe of His righteousness to clothe me.'

Then came the Crowning. At the Coronation of George VI the Archbishop could not work out which was the front of the Crown, as an over-enthusiastic aide had removed a little thread put there to identify it. This time the front was marked by a small gold star on the velvet, and there was no problem. The Archbishop takes up the story:

The putting on of the Crown went very smoothly. Having got the front edge at the right place on The Queen's forehead, I pressed the back down and then gave a slight gentle pressure in front. It looked all right to me, and by a glance from The Queen she indicated that it was all right. She confirmed it was quite steady.

The newly crowned Queen, holding the Rod and Sceptre, sits in the Coronation Chair as the choir sing the anthem – 'Be Strong and of a Good Courage'.

At this point the congregation shouted 'God Save The Queen', the trumpets sounded, the Abbey's bells rang out and, in accordance with the rubric in the Order of Service, 'The great guns at the Tower shall be shot off.' As the acclamation subsided, the Archbishop sealed the act with the words 'God crown you with a crown of glory and righteousness, that having a right faith and manifold fruit of good works, you may obtain the crown of an everlasting kingdom by the gift of him whose kingdom endureth for ever.'

At the moment of Crowning the peers and peeresses put on their coronets, which had been delivered to them just before by their pages, who had been sitting on the steps close by between the blocks of seats. According to the page John Aird in his diary, 'They beat the Archbishop to it and put them on before the Archbishop crowned The Queen. The next five minutes on the peeresses' side was spent in violent prodding of hair pins through the coronet to keep it on.' The choir then sang the *Confortare* 'Be Strong and of a Good Courage' by Sir George Dyson, the words having been changed from the previous Coronation, when the opening words had been 'Be strong and play the man'.

Now, anointed and crowned, The Queen was escorted to her Throne, ready for the Homage. The Archbishop of Canterbury was the first to pledge he would be faithful and true, followed by the Duke of Edinburgh, kneeling at her feet. The dignity of the Homage was maintained until Baron Mowbray Segrave and Stourton came forward. After making his Homage he retreated and was, according to the Archbishop's account, all over the place, 'bunching up his robe and tripping over it and, as The Queen said, with mothballs and pieces of ermine flying in all directions'.

After the solemnity of the Homage came drums and a fanfare and a threefold shout from the congregation: 'God Save Queen Elizabeth, Long Live Queen Elizabeth, May The Queen Live For Ever'. The Archbishop had anticipated this might be tricky to cue, and so it was. There was an awkward pause. The Dean said later that he wondered whether he should start the shouting, but eventually William McKie signalled the choir to lead the way. Later the Archbishop said that the drums, fanfare and shouts had come in the wrong place. They should have come immediately after the enthroning, once the Archbishop had said, 'Stand firm and hold fast from henceforth the seat and state of royal and imperial dignity' etc. '*There* should come the drums, a brief fanfare and cries of Long Live etc.', he wrote. 'By the time the end of the Homage comes it is impossible to work up again the vocal enthusiasm necessary for the cries: the excitement has passed and cannot be revived.'

With the Homage over, the Communion service resumed with the Offertory, during which The Queen made her gift or Oblation: an altar cloth and an ingot of gold weighing 1 pound (45 grams). At the final rehearsal the Earl Marshal had made it clear that everything was to be done on the day exactly as at the final rehearsal, with no deviations. Perhaps the Dean had not heard. The ingot was to be placed in a small basin held for her by the Archbishop, but at the last minute he discovered that the Dean had substituted a huge alms dish, which sat precariously on the corner of the altar and was at risk of toppling over. According to the Archbishop, it was 'a really vast thing on which to put a little bag containing a tiny weight of gold. I could only just lift it with my hands wide apart.' It was heavily embossed, and when it was the Duke's turn to place his gift – a silver box – on it, he could not find a flat surface for it 'and it slipped to and fro.' The Archbishop was not pleased. 'It was monstrous of the Dean to spring this on me without any warning.'

According to Garter King of Arms, The Queen's ingot of gold (2 inches by 1 inch by ¼ of an inch thick) would make 'a perfectly charming paperweight', although he had no doubt the Dean would put it to better use. In 1937 King George's gift of gold had been used to help gild

The Queen, surrounded by peers and bishops, waits for the Homage to begin.

the choir stalls. The Queen's gift is thought to have been put towards the Abbey's Coronation Appeal for the upkeep of the fabric. The altar frontal The Queen was due to give had not been finished, so a token piece of embroidered cloth was substituted; the frontal itself did not arrive until two years later. In his 'Book of Private Devotions' the Archbishop had written explaining how The Queen should view the gifts: 'I shall offer an altar cloth and a weight of gold, signifying that not only the common labours of the earth but also the works of art and beauty and of exquisite skills are to be offered to God and used to his glory and the good of his people.'

After The Queen and the Duke of Edinburgh had taken Communion, during which the Choir sang Vaughan Williams's 'O Taste and See', came Sir Charles Stanford's *Gloria* followed by the Blessing. The Coronation was nearly over, and The Queen retired into her 'traverse' (St Edward's Chapel, behind the altar screen) to exchange St Edward's Crown for the Imperial State Crown and to put on her exquisite robe of purple velvet. Her maids of honour went with her, and Lady Glenconner remembers that, once out of view, the Bishop of Bath and Wells produced a flask of brandy and offered them reviving sips.

While this was going on, the choir sang William Walton's lengthy *Te Deum*, which the Archbishop later criticised for being too long: 'The *Te Deum* should be sung with reverent attention – but inside the Abbey nobody is paying any attention to the words or their meaning.' In future, he believed, the *Te Deum* should be omitted from the service altogether.

In the procession out, Simon Benton Jones, page to the Duke of Richmond and Gordon, was walking ahead of The Queen. 'My mother and nanny had been worried in case my buckled shoes fell off and tripped The Queen up. So they tied them on with elastic and all was well.'

The Coronation was over. Despite many reservations expressed earlier about the suitability of the ancient rite in the mid-twentieth century, its impact was remarkable. The Archbishop felt its religious significance had been much more generally appreciated than at the Coronation of George VI. 'I think The Queen's request for the prayers of everybody in her Christmas broadcast made a very deep impression.'

The Dean in his account wrote that The Queen 'had played her part with great simplicity and without any trace of nervousness or self-consciousness'. He also praised her supporting bishops: 'Durham, aged under 50, yet looking as venerable as a septuagenarian, and Bath and Wells, not good-looking but full of solicitude for The Queen, performed with conspicuous skill.'

Even those who might have taken a rather cynical view were won over. Several people told the Archbishop that the Soviet Ambassador, Yacob Malik, had his attention riveted on the service all the time, 'with a look on his face of a kind of sadness that this was something outside himself'. Even the Papal envoy, who had refused a seat in the Abbey but had a seat in the stand opposite the Annexe, and who had followed the service by loudspeaker, declared it 'très spirituelle'.

Wearing her robe of purple velvet, the Queen processes through the nave after her Coronation, her maids of honour bearing her train.

CHAPTER 6

Relief and celebration

As THE QUEEN'S PROCESSION ENTERED the Annexe at the end of the service, there was an excited buzz of conversation as those in the congregation anticipated their exit from the Abbey and, for many, much-needed refreshments arranged by the Ministry of Works at various nearby venues. The Queen and the Royal Family did not have far to go for their lunch, as the Duke of Edinburgh's robing room in the Annexe had been transformed into the royal dining room, with tables and chairs bought especially for the event, although the lunch nearly did not happen as the staff bringing it from Buckingham Palace had forgotten their security passes and had to talk their way in.

An hour later The Queen, rested and refreshed, re-entered her golden coach for the long procession back to the Palace. Two of her maids of honour followed her in the procession to help with her train at the Palace; the other four were taken direct to the Palace by police car. But first, Baroness Willoughby de Eresby remembers being allowed into the royal dining room to finish what remained of the food. 'The Queen had hardly touched the food, which she had no appetite for because she must have been exhausted. It was a very unexpected treat – very good fresh fish and the most delicious white wine.' Meanwhile the royal procession wound its way on a five-mile route back to the Palace along Whitehall, through Admiralty Arch and then via Pall Mall, St James's Street, Piccadilly, Hyde Park Corner, Park Lane, Oxford Street, Regent Street, Haymarket, back through Admiralty Arch and down the Mall to Buckingham Palace. The journey took an hour and forty minutes, and the thousands who lined the route, many having camped out for two or three nights to get a good vantage point, were not disappointed. The procession was two miles long and took forty-five minutes to pass any one point. Ten thousand servicemen took part, including detachments from the Solomon Islands, North Borneo, Sarawak, Malaya, Bermuda, Trinidad, Malta, Cyprus, West Africa and Singapore and Colonial troops from Ceylon, Pakistan, South Africa, New Zealand and

Hurrying to escape the rain, peers in their coronets make for the House of Lords after the service.

Canada. Forty-six bands were either in the procession or along the route. The Queen, wearing her Crown, happily waved in response to the deafening cheers.

As The Queen's carriage turned into the gates of the Palace, the crowds surged forward to wait once more, this time for the balcony appearance, although that would not be for an hour or so. First there were the formal photographs, to be taken by Cecil Beaton. The Queen was asked whether she was happy for them to be taken then or whether she wanted to postpone the session to a later day. According to Baroness Willoughby de Eresby, 'She decided that as she was all dressed up she wanted it done there and then.'

While everyone waited for the photography to begin, Michael Anson and The Queen Mother's other pages, who had also been taken by police car to the Palace, helped The Queen Mother entertain the young Prince Charles and Princess Anne.

They suggested they would like to ride in her train like a wheelbarrow, so we went galloping up and down the passages with The Queen Mother thinking it was a wonderful joke, with these two little people jumping on and off the train as we carried it with them sitting in the middle. The Queen Mother was really up for it.

The photography was an exacting process, with the maids of honour working hard in response to Cecil Beaton's instructions on how to arrange the train. Then came the balcony appearance before the thousands in front of the Palace and crowding the Mall. According to Baroness Willoughby de Eresby, 'That was immense fun and quite unexpected for us. People were shouting and cheering as far as the eye could see towards Trafalgar Square.' Michael Anson and the other pages had held back, but The Queen Mother insisted that they too should go on to the balcony. 'That really was an incredible experience, looking down on all

Wearing the Imperial State Crown, The Queen begins her long procession back to Buckingham Palace.

these people,' he said. Photographs in the newspapers the next day show him standing between The Queen and the Duke of Edinburgh. Later, with the crowds still cheering, there was another balcony appearance – this time without the maids of honour. Baroness Willoughby de Eresby recalls: 'By now The Queen had taken off her train. Someone had rolled it up and moved it out of the way and no one could find it, so our justification for going out had gone, and we had to stay behind.'

At previous Coronations there had been long delays for those leaving the Abbey, as their exit had to be co-ordinated with the arrival of their chauffeur-driven cars. For some, notably a group of distinguished American reporters sitting in the north transept, a swift exit was essential, as they had to transmit their accounts of the service to their newspapers thousands of miles away. But an over-zealous Gold Staff Officer, a Brigadier, refused to allow them to leave

promptly, despite increasingly desperate pleadings. A formal complaint made later by the Association of American Correspondents to the Chief Gold Staff Officer resulted in him castigating his junior for acting 'extremely tactlessly and contrary to instructions'.

As the Abbey emptied, cleaners, firemen, vergers and Ministry of Works officials swept through the church, snapping up the spare Orders of Service and other souvenirs and gathering up lost property, including a diamond necklace, which was not claimed for six weeks. There had been a certain amount of treasure-hunting. Someone had cut the embroidered

Many thousands of people camped out along the route in the rain to ensure they got a good view of The Queen as she returned home.

The crowds waited ten deep in places to cheer as the golden coach passed by.

royal cipher from one of the peers' chairs, and a piece of blue silk frontal from the tiers of seats had been cut away. The Ministry had planned to take a comprehensive series of photographs showing the Abbey exactly as it had been set up for the Coronation. There had been no time to do it before the day itself, because it was either unfinished or being used for rehearsals. To the Ministry's dismay they could not do it immediately afterwards either, because there was so much litter, including sandwich wrappers, napkins and empty bottles under the chairs – mainly miniature gin and brandy bottles where the peeresses had been sitting and whisky bottles where the peers had sat.

The next day preparations began for the official opening of the Abbey so that the public could see it in its Coronation setting, so once again the photographs had to be postponed. By

The two-mile long procession took forty-five minutes to pass any one point. The Mall was spanned by triumphal arches with golden crowns beneath.

The Queen, Prince Charles, Princess Anne and The Duke of Edinburgh appeared on the balcony to acknowledge the cheers of the crowd and watch a flypast.

the time the pictures were taken, the Abbey was no longer exactly as it had been for the service. One item that had gone missing was the small stool on which the peers had knelt when making their Homage, and despite inquiries by Special Branch it could not be found. Garter King of Arms advertised in the press, and eventually it was posted anonymously to Scotland Yard. It was then sent to Arundel Castle as part of the Earl Marshal's perquisites.

A few days after the Coronation a play opened at the Abbey to help raise money for its restoration appeal. It starred several well-known actors and set many others on the road to stardom. The Coronation theatre was transformed into the stage, a backdrop was erected concealing the altar and the Coronation Chair, and The Queen's Throne was removed for the performances. Written by Christopher Hassall, *Out of the Whirlwind* was more a pageant than

The photographs taken in the Throne Room of Buckingham Palace after the Coronation included this large group of The Queen's extended family.

Moments before this photograph was taken the young Princess Anne and Prince Charles had been riding up and down the Palace corridors in the Queen Mother's train, held by her pages.

a play and was not well received by the critics, but the star of the show was the setting, and it was a sell-out for its three-week run – even The Queen Mother came. The music was provided by the Abbey's choristers, who began each performance by processing through the backdrop as though at the end of Evensong. While behind the scenes and out of sight, several had amused themselves by sitting in the Coronation Chair. One of the boys, Gordon Nixon, had also sat in the Coronation Coach when it was parked in Dean's Yard during a Coronation rehearsal (he reported it was not very plush and was rather disappointing compared with the outside) and must be the only person other than The Queen to have sat in both.

After three weeks the play closed, and soon it was time to close the Abbey for the whole apparatus of Coronation to be removed. It was November before the Abbey was returned to the Dean and Chapter in the same condition as it had been surrendered.

One of the major successes of the Coronation was the television coverage, which defied all the earlier official reservations. The Dean said that his misgivings had been entirely allayed: 'One was quite unconscious of any disturbance and oblivious of the fact that millions of eyes were watching the proceedings.' The Archbishop of Canterbury said that the religious impact of the service had been immense, even though he still regarded television as 'an extravagance and a supreme time-waster'. But even the Dean and the Archbishop perhaps did not realise at the time how big the impact of the coverage had been. It ushered in the television age. It was the largest operation the BBC had ever mounted; the number of television sets sold soared; and it is estimated that half the population of the country watched the Coronation live on television.

One of the keys to its success was the role played by the commentator in the Abbey, Richard Dimbleby, who was secreted in the triforium above the east end. His meticulous research and timing shepherded the viewer through the ceremony without intruding on any words spoken by The Queen or the Archbishop, although inevitably he talked over some of the music.

The television feed was taken by France, the Netherlands and West Germany. American networks recorded the BBC's pictures from the Abbey and made complicated arrangements to ferry their recordings across the Atlantic by aircraft for re-broadcast (there were no satellite relays in those days). Intensely competitive, they spared no cost to beat their rivals, and that evening 85 million Americans watched a British monarch being crowned.

Never before had a Coronation had such an international impact. In previous centuries, when the monarch was all-powerful, the Coronation was essentially an almost private affair. Now, with a constitutional monarch shorn of political power, the Coronation could not have been more public. Today, sixty years later, that remarkable day is still remembered by those who were there, and by the many millions who witnessed it at home.

The formal photograph of The Queen and The Duke of Edinburgh has echoes of official Coronation portraits from previous centuries.

Afterword

Personal memories of participants in the Coronation have helped to bring the story alive. I was four at the time of the Coronation of Queen Elizabeth II and still vividly remember the wider family crowding round our grandparents' small television set. There were so many families like ours throughout the land. These reflections naturally lead to a moment's thought about the Coronation's significance.

The moment of Coronation is the high point of a religious ceremony that focuses on the duty of the Monarch towards God and the people. Before being invested with priestly robes and being handed the Orb and other Regalia, The Queen – under a great canopy to conceal the sacred moment – was anointed with holy oil just as the Bible tells us Saul, David and Solomon were anointed kings of Israel. Our Lord Jesus himself is 'the anointed one', the meaning of the Greek word 'Christ'. The Coronation service concludes with the reception of Holy Communion, which enables the communicant to become more like Jesus Christ: 'Grant us therefore, gracious Lord … that we may evermore dwell in him, and he in us.' The Monarch is called to follow the example of Jesus, who came 'not to be served but to serve, and to give his life a ransom for many', and sets a pattern of servant leadership for the whole nation.

At her Coronation The Queen was set apart and strengthened for service to her people and to God. That commitment was, of course, not new. In 1947, on her twenty-first birthday, the then Princess Elizabeth had committed herself to the service of the people of the Commonwealth and her reliance on God's help: 'I declare before you all that my whole life whether it be long or short shall be devoted to your service … God help me to make good my vow, and God bless all of you who are willing to share in it.'

The Abbey has long represented the place of the Church in the fabric of our system of government. The Abbey houses the Shrine of St Edward the Confessor, King of England from 1042 to 1066, humble servant of God and of his people, who built a great church for the Abbey beside his Palace of Westminster. Ever since 1066, kings and queens have been crowned here in an essentially unchanging manner. Thus, at the heart of our nation's story, Church and State have been side by side, down the centuries, often best when challenging one another but essentially working together to root this nation in the value of service.

Sixty years after the Coronation, we celebrate and give thanks to God for the faithful service of God and her people The Queen has offered and exemplified throughout her reign.

The Very Reverend Dr John Hall,
Dean of Westminster

Index

© Scala Publishers Ltd, 2011
Text © James Wilkinson and
Westminster Abbey Enterprises Ltd, 2011

First published in 2011 by
Scala Publishers Ltd
Northburgh House
10 Northburgh Street
London EC1V OAT, UK
www.scalapublishers.com

ISBN 978-1-85759-735-6

Project editor: Esme West
Proofreader: Julie Pickard
Designer: Nigel Soper
Printed and bound in China

10 9 8 7 6 5 4 3 2 1

British library Cataloguing
in Publication Data
A catalogue record for this book
is available from the British Library

Acknowledgements

I would like to acknowledge the help of the Dean and Chapter of
Westminster, Sir Stephen Lamport, Sir John Aird, Sir Simon Benton
Jones, Dr Robert Charles, Mr Michael Willoughby, Mr Gavin Ross,
Lord Cranworth, the Rt Hon. the Baroness Willoughy de Eresby,
Lady Glenconner, Sir Henry Keswick, Mr Michael Anson, His Grace the
Duke of Devonshire, Mr John Whitworth, Dr C.S. Knighton, Dr Richard
Mortimer, the Keeper of the Muniments at Westminster Abbey, and
Miss Christine Reynolds, the Assistant Keeper. Extracts from the papers
of Geoffrey Fisher, Archbishop of Canterbury (vols 123–5), are published
by permission of the Trustees of Lambeth Palace Library. I would also
like to thank the Librarian of the College of Arms, Mr Robert Yorke, for
allowing me to see the College's extensive collection of papers relating
to the Coronation, and Dr John Martin Robinson, Librarian to the
Duke of Norfolk, for allowing me access to the Earl Marshal's papers.
JAMES WILKINSON

PHOTOGRAPHIC CREDITS:
pp. 22–3 © Alpha Library, 2011
front cover © Beaton / Camera Press London, 2011
p. 26 © Bridgeman Art Library, 2011
pp. 12–3 © Dean and Chapter of Westminster Abbey, 2011
pp. 2, 14, 17, 21, 25, 27 (left and right), 28, 29, 31, 39, 41, 43, 47, 48, 49, 53,
54, 55 (top and bottom), 57, 58 © Getty Images, 2011
pp. 1, 32, 33, 34 © Historic Royal Palaces, 2011
p. 9 © Karsh / Camera Press London, 2011
pp. 10, 11, 40, 45, 51, 56 © Press Association, 2011
inside cover, pp. 7, 35–7 The Royal Collection © 2011 Her Majesty Queen
Elizabeth II
back cover © www.royalimages.co.uk
pp. 18–9 © Sir Henry Rushbury / John Mowlem, 2011
p. 4 © Alan Shawcross / Anthony Buckley & Constantine, 2011
pp. 59, 61 © Victoria & Albert Museum, 2011

PAGE ONE:
A cross of red rubies overlays a large sapphire
in the Sovereign's Ring, put on the fourth finger
of the Queen's right hand during the Investiture.

FRONTISPIECE:
The Queen's husband, The Duke of Edinburgh,
pledges to become 'your liege man of life and limb'
as he makes his Homage.